Praise for
Rolling Pin Devotions:

The author does a terrific job taking everyday
items and pointing us to Jesus and the Bible.
The scripture references are a bonus,
encouraging us to read deeper.
The illustrations are an added enjoyment!
~ Tina B.

I love how the author gently reminds us
that times will be difficult,
but to look at what's in front of us.
~ Sherry R.

Rolling Pin Devotions

By Marissa Barbee

Illustrated by Miriam Teramura

Scripture quotations are from The ESV® Bible (The Holy Bible, English Standard Version®), © 2001 by Crossway, a publishing ministry of Good News Publishers. Used by permission. All rights reserved.

ISBN 979-8-9935951-0-8

To my precious daughters,
whether by the bond of blood or of love,
may your cup run over!

Olivia ~

As a fun, visual reminder of a cup that runs over
and in honor of you and your love of coffee
these illustrations were painted with your
favorite beverage.

Table of Contents

The
Cup

You prepare a table before me
in the presence of my enemies;
you anoint my head with oil;
my cup overflows.
~Psalm 23:5

"Wow, your hands are full!" I began hearing comments like this one when our third child was born and I had three precious children aged three and under. As each additional child arrived—each a blessing to our family—these comments became increasingly frequent. They never really required a response, but they caused me to think, and these thoughts were likely much deeper than the commenter had any intention of going. Of course, my life and my hands were busy. It is a lot of work to properly teach and train even one child, let alone nine children who are at nine different stages of life with nine different sets of needs. But the blessings that were and are mine as their mother are beyond description! My favorite thing is observing how my children interact with one another. As each child's personality developed, I could see that they all approached and responded to their brothers and sisters differently. They were forming distinct, individualistic relationships with each other. Each personality added variety and depth to our family. Needless to say, my heart has always been far more full than my hands. Truly, my cup overflows!

Of course, there have also been times when the trials weighed heavily on me; when wounds from hurts and betrayals cut painfully deep; when finances were tight; when life's waves rushed in and threatened to overtake me. In those times it was crucial for me to deliberately and consistently name and count my blessings—

something my heart sometimes resisted at first. There were times when I sat in tears with a precious little one on my lap and other concerned little faces looking up at me, and the love I received from my little ones started my count: "Thank you, Lord, for the blessing of these little ones around me." Inevitably, by the time I reached the exceedingly great number of ten, my entire perspective had changed as I realized that even in the heaviest of trials the blessings from my Heavenly Father outweighed the momentary challenges, even if they were a little harder to focus on. God always provided for our needs, sometimes in unexpected ways. The peace that passes understanding was always available, hope and purpose were never far away. I knew that my cup of joy would soon be overflowing again!

As I put these thoughts down in writing, I am praying for you, dear reader, to begin and continue to name and count your many blessings—past and present—from your Heavenly Father. Count them on the good days when it comes easy and count them especially on the hard and difficult days—even if it is just a sweet smile from a little one or an encouraging smile from a stranger. Start counting. Keep counting. Count until you find your cup of blessing overflows.

Digging Deeper:

Psalm 23:1-6; Proverbs 16:20; Jeremiah 29:11; Lamentations 3:22-23; John 10:7-18; Romans 8:28; Ephesians 1:3; 3:14-21; Philippians 4:4-7; 1 Timothy 1:12-17; 1 Peter 3:14-16

Challenge:

How do these verses encourage you? There is no question that the Lord's love for you is abundant at every moment of your life! One constant blessing we experience when we belong to him is eternal safety and security within his flock. With the Lord as your Shepherd your cup is bound to overflow, even in the presence of your enemies.

The
Calendar

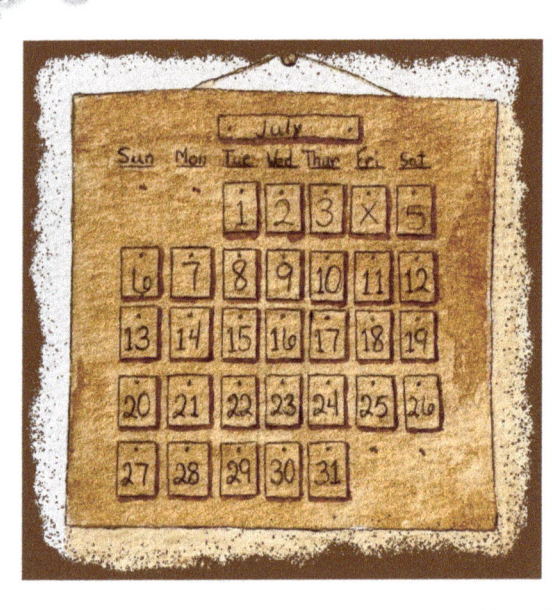

*The plans of the diligent
lead surely to abundance,
but everyone who is hasty
comes only to poverty.*
~Proverbs 21:5

I am a planner! I rely on calendars, lists, and systems. I start packing for a trip at least a month in advance. If there are supplies or gifts to take along, I collect those items into one area as soon as the trip is scheduled. Because of dietary needs, I plan menus and make lists a good month ahead of any trip as I figure out what will be available for food preparation at our destination; what ingredients I need to pack versus what I can get when we arrive. Should the meals be grab-and-go or foods that do not require refrigeration? I begin packing clothes as soon as I do laundry the week before the trip, so I can avoid a last-minute rush to wash and dry a needed item. As our family grew, planning got to be even more extensive!

This tendency of mine to begin packing a month before a trip surprised my husband after we got married. I was equally surprised by his comfort level with last-minute packing. He can wait until a couple of hours before departure to gather available clothes from the closet and check his list for things he may have jotted down to remember. We certainly have distinctive styles, but we both plan since both of us have a list. After 24 years, we still chuckle at these differences anytime we begin planning for a trip.

The wise person knows the necessity of planning. As we read in Luke chapter 14, it is important to sit down and count the cost in all things, to plan ahead rather than charge ahead. In this scripture, Jesus gives us practical examples to illustrate the importance of understanding the cost of following Him. When we belong to Him, we need to make all our plans secondary to His will, being ready to cancel or modify our plans or have them interrupted for His purpose.

Sometimes the Lord takes us through hard things—things which are not part of our plan. Jeremiah 29:11 says, "For I know the plans I have for you, declares the LORD, plans for welfare and not for evil, to give you a future and a hope." This is not a promise for a life of ease. After all, God is sending his people into captivity. This is the promise that He has a purpose, despite what plans are derailed and what trials we face. He is directing our path, lovingly teaching, guiding, preparing, and sanctifying us.

We must remain vigilant in our planning, sensitive to the spirit, and ready to move where God is sending us. Paul wrote several times about how his plans were prevented. If our plans are in line with God's, he does not fail to make a way. When in doubt cling to the promise given to us in Proverbs 3:5-6, "Trust in the LORD with all your heart, and do not lean on your own understanding. In all your ways acknowledge him, and he will make straight your paths."

Digging Deeper:

Proverbs 3:5-8, 27:1; Isaiah 55:8-11; Luke 12:18-23, 14:25-33; Acts 16:6-10; Romans 1:13, 15:22; 1 Thessalonians 2:17-18; James 4:13-15

Challenge:

When your plans get derailed, how do you respond? Is your response disappointment or discouragement? Counteract this by developing the habit of searching out God's plan and purpose both in the smallest and the largest of derailed plans. Watch with expectation for what He is doing instead!

The
Rolling Pin

*...not by the way of eye-service,
as people-pleasers, but as bondservants of
Christ, doing the will of God from the heart,
rendering service with a good will as to the
Lord and not to man...*

~Ephesians 6:6-7

My first word was "taste." I loved to watch my mother roll out the dough for our morning biscuits while waiting for a taste of the leftover dough. Growing up I admired the ease with which she worked the dough. It always seemed such a simple task for her to get the dough to do exactly what she wanted. When I verbalized these thoughts to her one day, her reply was not what I had expected. Instead of thanking me and offering words of wisdom in training, she lamented that she was not as talented with a rolling pin as her grandmother was.

Then came the day when it was my daughter's turn to stand in awe as I rolled the dough for our breakfast biscuits. The little girl standing beside me saw "perfection" and "ease" in the work I was doing. I honestly do not recall my response to her words of admiration, but I remember having a difficult time accepting her childlike awe. I only saw my imperfections and felt frustration that I still could not manage the dough like my mom. Over the years as I continue to roll dough to feed my family, God has repeatedly brought these memories to mind, encouraging me to look to Him as my only standard.

We tend to compare ourselves to others in just about every area of life: homemaking, parenting, educational choices, marriage, income level, cars, our dress, style, and how we look. I have even found myself comparing my spiritual life and growth to that of others. We are meant to compare and evaluate ourselves, but only when we are using the standards and measurements given to us by God. 1 Corinthians (10:31-11:1) tells us that our only standard is what brings glory to God and what he proclaims about us. When we replace that standard with the benchmark of our neighbor, the influencer on social media, or even our own ideals, we have entered dangerous waters. Exchanging of standards is a clue that Satan has taken and twisted for his own evil purpose the good standards which are given by God. When we trade God's standard, attitudes of judgment and condemnation are sure to follow. If these attitudes are not directed toward oneself, they are directed toward others. Once we are in these dangerous waters, Satan attacks by either stroking our ego or cutting us down through condemnation. Neither pleases the Lord!

Comparing my rolling pin skills with Mom's illustrates how we evaluate things differently from others and how our judgment is clouded when our standard is wrong. When our standard is to do everything in such a way as to bring honor and glory to the Lord, we get a taste of the Lord's goodness because judgment and condemnation are dissolved. In their place we find opportunities for growth and ministry.

Digging Deeper:

1 Samuel 16 (esp. verse 7); Psalm 139:13-16; Matthew 10:26-33; Romans 5:8; 2 Corinthians 5:16-21, 12:9; Philippians 4:8

Challenge:

Think of the times when you are quick to begin comparing yourself to others. How does that affect your sense of worth? Are these thoughts God-honoring? Commit to fighting the tendency to compare yourself to others with thoughts that are true, honorable, just, and pure. Let your sense of worth and value be firmly established in what God says about you as his child.

The
Sewing Kit

Be angry and do not sin; do not let the sun go down on your anger, and give no opportunity to the devil.

~Ephesians 4:26-27

"A stitch in time saves nine." I have tested this well-known adage and can affirm it is true. A loose button which could be secured in a moment can turn into a missing button. A subsequent futile search for it may be followed by an even more extensive search for a suitable replacement. Procrastination is costly. It can turn minutes of neglected repairs into hours of belated reconstruction. To fix a loose seam or a small tear would take but a moment. But if I ignore it and first wash the garment, that small tear becomes larger, the small opening at the seam unravels, and I end up having a garment that is not only more difficult to repair but may have become unfit for repair.

This proverb is applicable in other areas as well. Ignoring a small leak in a faucet can ruin a cabinet or eventually lead to rotting floorboards. Disregarding the need for a simple oil change in the car can turn into the need for a complete engine change. Forgetting to save a document online has cost many students and professionals hours of additional work redoing assignments.

Perhaps you have experienced the momentary pain of removing a small splinter as well as the continuous pain of a festering wound from a splinter left in place. Similarly, our relationships can suffer breakdowns when minor issues, hurts, and frustrations are left to fester and swell. In a world of sinful, broken people, misunderstandings, offensive words, and wounding actions are inevitable. In such situations we are called to humble ourselves and first search ourselves to find out if we have done wrong. On the other hand, we are also called to graciously confront others in love rather than anger. Both are difficult steps to take, but the way we handle broken relationships speaks volumes.

Broken relationships dishonor our Lord. And the world is watching how we handle them, whether we like it or not. The world is evaluating the truth of what we say by what we do, that is by how we love one another (John 13:31-35). In light of this, God gives us specific instructions on how to heal relationships quickly, whether we are being offended or are the offender. Pursuing a quick restoration of lost rapport with loved ones, those in the body of Christ, or a neighbor (Luke 10:29-37) is far easier than trying to mend such relationships in the future when wounds have deepened and resentment has grown. This is a difficult calling, but in God's economy "the stitch in time" holds true as well and can prevent large-scale tears in the precious relationships within the body of Christ.

Digging Deeper:

Psalm 37:8; Proverbs 15:1; Matthew 5:21-26 and 18:15-20; Ephesians 4:1-32; James 3:13-4:12; 1 Peter 3:8-22; Romans 15:5-7; Col. 3:12-14

Challenge:

Communication is the fabric of relationships. The work of restoring broken relationships is hard and humbling. Whenever you experience pain or anger regarding a relationship, first ask the Lord for his input and counsel. Ponder the above passages and ask the Lord to help you make that necessary stitch quickly and wisely in order to prevent more harm, increased hurt, and greater damage.

The
Cast Iron Skillet

Not only that, but we rejoice in our sufferings, knowing that suffering produces endurance, and endurance produces character, and character produces hope, and hope does not put us to shame, because God's love has been poured into our hearts through the Holy Spirit who has been given to us.

~Romans 5:3–5

Cast iron cookware, blackened by use and age, has a rich history. If that skillet could talk it might tell you of all the heat it has endured over the years, the many flavors concocted and the many meals prepared and enjoyed by generations of family and friends. It witnessed joyful family celebrations, monotonous day-to-day preparations, and pain-filled occasions when the cook sobbed and cried while stirring the ingredients.

Cast iron consists of a peculiar, enduring material. It is tough as nails and it's very difficult to completely ruin it. The more it is used the blacker it becomes and the less food will stick to the pan. Seasoning the skillet is beneficial and is accomplished at the cost of time and high heat that burns the oils deep into the cast iron. Occasionally the seasoning gets stripped away by acidic foods or the need to remove firmly stuck food particles causes superficial abrasions. With proper care, the seasoning is restored as the pan is exposed to more oils and heat, showcasing the skillet's enduring usefulness.

Pondering the nature of cast iron, we can discover a lesson for the believer in Christ. As we face and endure the heat of trials, we are being seasoned by our loving, faithful God. He gently prepares us making certain the heat we face leads to positive results. At times we face trials so difficult we feel that all our seasoning is being stripped away. But God is ever present with his wise and tender care to heal, restore, and season us.

And Jesus—who endured all kinds of temptations and suffered death for us because he loves us so much—does not minimize what we are going through and struggling with but actually enters into it with us. As we keep our eyes on Him, He gives us the strength to endure with him to the end.

When trials and tribulations strike, take courage as you consider the humble cast iron skillet. The more heat it endures, the more useful it becomes to those who rely on it. Our loving Heavenly Father knows exactly how best to care for us and develop our capabilities. Each trial has the potential to make us more usable in his kingdom, as we are seasoned to serve those around us in His name and for His glory.

Digging Deeper:

Matthew 10:22; Romans 5:3-4; 1 Corinthians 10:13; Galatians 6:9; Hebrews 12:1-17; James 1:1-12

Challenge:

Consider what you have endured and struggled through in the past. What trials and difficulties are you experiencing right now? How do you think these difficulties have seasoned you for the Lord's work? Do you know anyone who needs to hear your story to help them endure a similar trial? If no one comes to mind right now, ask the Lord to introduce you to that person.

The Rag

And we know that for those who love God all things work together for good, for those who are called according to his purpose.
~Romans 8:28

In preparation for our marriage, my husband and I created a gift registry. The possibilities of what to add to the list seemed endless. There were so many fun and pleasant things. We thought about how we wanted our home to look, how to organize it, and how to host people. We listed what we had, what we needed, and what would be nice to have. Then we created our wedding registry accordingly.

When I opened the gifts at my bridal shower, I recognized a lot of those items. It was fun to see how the life we were dreaming of was beginning to take shape. Then I opened a gift which I will never forget. This item was not on my registry, nor have I ever seen it listed on any other registry. It was a neatly folded pile of rags, beautifully tied together, with a handwritten note that said, "A bride never knows the importance of rags until she finds that she does not have any." Those rags were the most memorable gift I received. Not only because of the frequency with which they were put to use, but also because of the wisdom I recognized in the gift giver.

While rags are not particularly pretty, they are absolutely necessary. They change in time from being a nice set of towels to ragged, worn and thin threads which we would never offer to a guest. But we do not throw them away, either. In this state, they take on a very different but key role in the home. These rags get used for the really grimy jobs for which we would never use our nice towels. At the beginning of married life, we have not had time or opportunity to wear out any cloths or towels. But we do have a choice: Humbly accept them from someone with experience or use the nice ones.

Life can be messy and not just in the physical realm. Am I equipped for the cleanup? Is my faith so "well used" that I can fall back on it when trials and tribulations come and life feels messy? Will my familiarity with Scripture and my experience of God's faithfulness carry me through? Am I willing to lean on others? We all face times in life when we simply do not have the needed wisdom or depth of faith to get us through a particular mess. That is why God has put us in a community with other believers and has enabled someone to walk this road before us. The community of believers has a treasury of "faith rags" available which can help us out of these messy times. They are not pretty because they resulted from dealing with hard things in life. It can be mortifying to accept and to share them, but when we do, God's family is blessed... and a little less messy.

Digging Deeper:

Titus 2:1-15; 1 Thessalonians 5:11-19; Hebrews 3:13

Challenge:

Is there a seasoned man or woman in the faith who will teach, train, urge, admonish, encourage, and build you up? Someone whose faith has been tried and found strong, creating some of those spiritual rags? If not, ask God to provide someone like this for you.

On the flip side, are you being diligent in trusting God, learning through times of trial? What has God been teaching you? Are you willing to share your own faith rags to encourage others?

The
Mixing Bowl

Do not be unequally yoked with unbelievers. For what partnership has righteousness with lawlessness? Or what fellowship has light with darkness?

~2 Corinthians 6:14

If you are a baker, you can probably think of a time when you were adding ingredients to the mixing bowl and suddenly realized that you made a mistake. Perhaps you inadvertently added one ingredient twice or added a wrong ingredient. In any case, it was difficult to take out what had already been added. Your recipe was at a sudden standstill because now you had to figure out your best next steps. How could you salvage your recipe? Or at least salvage the ingredients?

The admonition not to be unequally yoked with an unbeliever is often applied to dating or marriage, but the context is much broader than that. Paul is telling the people of Corinth how important it is to separate themselves from the sinful things and practices of the world. If I view my life as a mixing bowl, I am adding all kinds of things to it. I need to be careful about paths I travel, habits I form, places I visit – physical as well as virtual. I need to choose carefully the company I keep and what I allow to enter into my home and family. The decisions we make regarding who and what we are mixing into our lives are often more far-reaching than we realize. Once we have added something to our lives, it is not easy to remove it. Our decisions—big and small— not only affect our lives, but also the lives of everyone around us.

We must be on guard because Satan is ever so eager to lead us astray. Behind the facade of things that might look innocent lurks the entrapment. To be perfectly honest, we must even exercise caution with regard to devotions we read and the Bible teachers we listen to. Everything we hear about the Word of God must be filtered through and measured by the entirety of scripture. In fact, the "digging deeper" section I include in every devotion is meant to be a tool for comparing what I say to God's recorded word.

When we stray—mixing something or someone into our lives that is not part of God's recipe—we need to remember that the God we serve is a God of redemption. Our next step should be confessing our shortcoming to the Lord and giving him the reins to guide us out of the situation we got ourselves into... and He will! He is second to none in taking what we give him, turning it around, and using it for his glory and our good!

Digging Deeper:

Proverbs 13:20; Ecclesiastes 4:9-12; Acts 17:10-12; Romans 8:28; 2 Corinthians 6:14-18; 1 Thessalonians 5:1-11; 1 Peter 5:8

Challenge:

Examine the mixing bowl of your life. What ingredients have been blended in? Are all ingredients intended by the Lord? Or are there some ingredients mixed in that do not honor and please him? Invite him to examine your life, purify and redeem it for his glory. Make the mixing bowl your continuous reminder of the importance of monitoring what you permit to enter into the mix of your life.

The
Basket

For my yoke is easy,
and my burden is light.
~Matthew 11:30

I love baskets – laundry baskets, picnic baskets, and blanket baskets! We use many different types of baskets in our home. Whether decorative or strictly utilitarian, baskets of every kind have one thing in common: They facilitate piling up and carrying different items at once.

Do you ever encounter times in your life when everything feels scattered and unusually heavy? In such moments I wish for some sort of life basket, a basket designed to hold and carry every aspect of life, neatly ordered, to help me manage and keep track of the various things God has entrusted to my care. What if I told you that there is such a basket?

When I was a nursing momma, I had a "quiet time basket". Its contents: a small Bible I could hold in one hand, a journal and a pen, and sometimes a Bible study book I was working through. It also had all the supplies I needed for baby feeding time: a diaper and wipes, a change of clothes, a burp cloth, and a nursing cover. Since I was not engaged in any other activities during feeding times, it was a terrific opportunity for me to spend time with the Lord. As soon as our little one got hungry, I grabbed the basket and settled down in a quiet place with the baby in my lap and the supply basket at my side. More often than not, however, my supplies stayed in the basket while I spent the time in prayer. During these quiet moments, I considered all the things that felt like heavy burdens, all the features of my life that appeared to be scattered and chaotic, and placed them one by one before the Lord. In this way, my "quiet time basket" morphed into my "life basket" where I collected my various life issues and laid them before the Lord, so he could take hold of, lift, and carry my burdens.

In a way, I was a lot like my toddlers were with their toy baskets. Just as they gathered their toys with my help into their toy baskets to restore order to our living area, I placed my concerns in the life basket with the help of my Lord. Throughout the day I might take a thing or two out, at other times I would empty the entire contents of the basket and scatter it far and wide with my worries.

God is a God of order. We were not meant to live our lives in chaos, stumbling under heavy burdens that affect our physical health and our spiritual peace. He offers to walk with us and help us carry our burdens every step of the way. He gives us rest in exchange for our burdens. That sounds too good to be true but is a divine gift promised us by God in his word.

Digging Deeper:

Psalms 34:17-19; 55:22; Isaiah 41:10-13; 46:3-4; Matthew 11:25-30; Philippians 4:4-9; 1 Peter 5:6-11; 1 John 5:1-5

Challenge:

Next time life feels heavy, chaotic, and scattered, grab your life basket and find a quiet place. Entrust all the things that are weighing you down to the Lord, one by one. Imagine placing each one back into the basket, then handing the basket to the Lord to let him carry it for you. In turn accept the rest and peace he offers you. Enjoy his burden which is light!

The Measuring Cup & Spoon

A full and fair weight you shall have, a full and fair measure you shall have, that your days may be long in the land that the LORD your God is giving you.

~Deuteronomy 25:15

Are you familiar with the saying, "Keeping score is a dangerous game"? Have you watched children happily playing with one another, then suddenly noticed a striking change in attitude, interaction, and camaraderie as soon as their play turns into a game that will have a winner and a loser? At this point arguments break out and the supervisor must assume the unwanted position of referee.

Unfortunately, this also happens in relationships when we begin to keep score. As soon as we have the impression that we are losing somehow, we assume a defensive posture and fight back. Thinking that something is not fair causes us to fight even harder to balance the equation as we see it. Then our love for one another changes from unconditional to conditional, with anger and resentment taking priority over gratitude and forgiveness.

In any relationship, keeping score leads to a continuous downward spiral which we must avoid by all means. If we take our hurts and frustrations to a third party, hoping to hear confirmation that we have indeed been wronged, that is a sure sign that we have stepped onto the court and are looking for the referee who will call "foul"–justifying a free shot. On the other hand, we could be sincerely seeking advice and direction from this person. We will know their level of wisdom in how they respond.

The one who responds by jumping into the role of referee is unwisely pushing us toward keeping score, while the one who encourages humble confrontation after a prayerful look into our own behavior and actions is helping us make sure our response is fully justified and fair.

We all want grace and forgiveness when we have done wrong. We want to continue to receive love and respect despite the times we have let others down. Keeping score is truly a dangerous game because it destroys relationships. When you have become the score keeper in your own game of life, it will be impossible to keep "full and fair weights" when relating to others because we can no longer accurately judge the scanty measure we use with others, while expecting a full and generous measure in return.

Do you detect growing resentment in any of your relationships? Are your relationships with parents, siblings, in-laws, your spouse, or even your children suffering from signs that you are keeping score of perceived wrongs you have endured? Ask the Lord to help you view things with a "full and fair weight" so that your response is above reproach.

Digging Deeper:

Proverbs 11:1; Matthew 7:12-14, 22:34-40; Luke 6:27-42; Colossians 3:12-14; 1 Peter 3:8-9; 1 John 2:7-11

Challenge:

Next time you feel anger or resentment rising in you, stop and take a step back. Double-check the measures you want to take. Are they "full and fair" or have they been skewed because you are about to step onto the court to settle the score? Ask the Lord to replace your skewed measures with his true measures.

The
Knife &
Cutting Board

*But now that you have been set free
from sin and have become slaves of God, the
fruit you get leads to sanctification
and its end, eternal life.*

~Romans 6:22

Knives and cutting boards are essential kitchen tools. The knife helps us remove unusable or undesirable parts of our food as well as give shape to the various ingredients of the meal. Depending on what we are trying to cut, this can be easy or difficult but is necessary and beneficial for the desired end product.

We can see similarities and can draw conclusions for our life in Christ. As new believers we are in a raw state. We have chosen to turn from sin and live for Christ and quickly realize that many of our old habits, desires, passions, and even some relationships either need to be cut or need a makeover on the Lord's cutting board where he can remove what is unsuitable and reshape what is acceptable. While the Lord cuts away the old, he also molds and shapes us to prepare us for service in his kingdom. He makes us holy which means "set apart for honorable use." That is not always a comfortable experience, no matter how you slice it!

We are talking about the process of sanctification. The apostle Paul experienced the cutting board and knife of sanctification in a serious way. He had plenty one day and was extremely poor the next; was sometimes moving around freely and locked away in chains at other times; tortured and stoned to the point of death, while also being honored as a spiritual father. Once Paul pleaded with the Lord to remove "a thorn in the flesh."

But what Paul considered undesirable, was actually something God had determined to use to sanctify Paul. We can see that through it all—the pleasant and the unpleasant—God fashioned Paul into the person he became, a chosen instrument in his eternal kingdom. Paul's biography can help us understand God's use of the knife and cutting board in our own lives so that we can also say with Paul, "... I have learned in whatever situation I am to be content." (Philippians 4:11)

Prompted by his love for us, God uses different ways to cut away the old and to shape and form us into that new person in Christ that is suitable for the work he has prepared for us in his kingdom. Of course, spending time on God's cutting board is not our first choice, and—like Paul—we might plead with the Lord for certain thorns or trials to be removed from us until we realize that we are learning to trust God much more while going through them, gaining strength continually. In hard times, I cling to the promise of Romans 8:28 because I know that the cutting board of life is really God at work molding and shaping me, working all things together for good according to his plans and purposes.

Digging Deeper:

John 17:17; Romans 6:1-23, 8:28, 12:2; 2 Corinthians 12: 7-10; Ephesians 5:25-27; Philippians 1:6, 2:12-13, 4:11-13; Hebrews 10:14; 1 Peter 1:13-16

Challenge:

As you use your knife and cutting board in the kitchen, consider how the Lord is sanctifying you. Your life may feel comfortable or uncomfortable right now or be a mixture of both. Even so, the Lord is using everything to mold and shape you. He has given you a place and a purpose in his kingdom. Can you see him preparing you? Can you see your place and purpose in his kingdom?

The
Clock

Look carefully then how you walk, not as unwise but as wise, making the best use of the time, because the days are evil.
~Ephesians 5:15–16

What, exactly, is time? The nature of time has been pondered by people across cultures and ages. An ancient Greek philosopher once said, "Time is the most valuable thing a man can spend." Thousands of years later, William Penn observed: "Time is what we want most, but what we use worst." Today, as parents, we keenly recognize how days can feel long and drawn out, while the years seem to fly by. We have captured this with the paradoxical saying, "The days are long, but the years are short."

Regrettably, many people do not grasp how significant the time is which they have been given until that time comes to an end. Some of the top regrets people have as they near the end of life: Valuing work more than family life; putting more effort into getting ahead financially and making the next promotion than investing in relationships; not forgiving an offense when they had the opportunity. The cost of investing in belongings over people or in choosing anger and bitterness instead of relational healing becomes painfully clear.

Today—the present time—is a gift. We are not promised tomorrow, but we are given the present moment to serve our Lord. It is far too easy to let the next thing become all-consuming when we listen to the overarching message the world gives: "You will be happy if and when…" Fill in any desire you might have: if and when you graduate...land the promotion...get married...the baby is born...you are able to focus on yourself...the kids are grown and flown...you reach retirement. We can continually miss out on the blessings of today if we neglect to identify them for the sake of future achievements and promises, which will keep contentment just out of reach. When we are not content with where God has us, it is difficult to serve him faithfully.

Benjamin Franklin, for all his idiosyncrasies, identified a crucial element of time when he said: "You may delay, but time will not." We can procrastinate in important matters, but time does not wait for us. Time cannot be reclaimed, repeated, or reserved. Time is a very precious thing the Lord entrusts us with. What do we do with it? In Matthew 25 our Lord tells us the parable of the servants who received talents from their master as he goes away. He expects them to invest the money and use it wisely for their master's benefit. We, too, have been given talents and the gift of time as we wait for the Lord's return or his calling us home. We are on mission for our Master and are called to live each day focused on whatever he places before us that day.

Digging Deeper:

Esther 4:14; Psalm 90:12; Proverbs 27:1; Ecclesiastes 3:1-8; John 9:4; Colossians 4:5-6; James 4:13-17; 1 John 2:17

Challenge:

"Count your blessings, count them one by one!" Whenever it is difficult for you to be content, count your blessings. This is a great reset which enables you to direct your focus onto everything the Lord has in store for you today. With this attitude you can use the gift of "today" wisely!

About The Author

Marissa Barbee finds joy in the parables and analogies of scripture, from the story of the potter and the clay found in Jeremiah to that of the salt and light of the world in the Gospels. Analogies have always played an important part in how Marissa understands, processes, and explains things. Over her many years of parenting Marissa has used everyday items, decorations, and sights to teach spiritual lessons to her children, pointing them to Christ every day through the everyday things around them. She now shares these modern day parables with you to encourage and strengthen your faith and to help you find Christ in the every day. Marissa and her husband, Scott, have raised their nine children in Colorado and together they savor every moment with their ever expanding family.

More by

More by
Marissa Barbee

Books:

- *Christmas Traditions Through the Lens of Scripture* - An advent devotional and Christmas countdown designed to help families find Christ in the common elements of the season.
- *Rolling Pin Devotions* - Turn your monotonous home management tasks into opportunities for spiritual reflection and growth with this series of devotions.
- *Find Christ in the Every Day* - This short devotional and workbook gives a framework for how to find Christ in your every day.

Other resources:

- *Finding Christ in the Midst of Halloween* - This brochure gives 31 ways to use fall decorations to help children focus on the messages of light and life offered by Christ over those of death and darkness offered by the world during this time of year.
- *Christmas Traditions: Cross Stitch Ornaments* - All 25 illustrations from the family advent devotion are converted into cross stitch patterns to make coordinating ornaments.

Visit MrsMarissaBarbee.com for more.

About The Illustrator

Miriam is an artist who enjoys transferring what she or others love onto paper or canvas. She works with a variety of mediums specific for the particular subject and project. Her favorite pieces are pencil pet or family portraits on paper. She also enjoys painting with acrylics, watercolors, or coffee when creating landscapes or still life subjects. Miriam is a busy mother and homemaker but still finds time to use and hone the artistic skills God has blessed her with.

More by
Miriam Teramura

Illustrated books:
- *Christmas Traditions Through the Lens of Scripture* by Marissa Barbee
- *Rolling Pin Devotions,* by Marissa Barbee
- *Finding Christ in the Every Day* by Marissa Barbee
- *A Ring for Two Queens* by William Adams

Other resources and places to find Miriam's art:
- *Christmas Traditions - A Coloring Companion*
- MrsMarissaBarbee.com
- Custom landscapes, portraits, and pet portraits

Visit PaintingInFrames.com to find out more.

www.ingramcontent.com/pod-product-compliance
Lightning Source LLC
Chambersburg PA
CBHW051647120626
46551CB00015B/2255